Fascinating Fruits

WAYLAND

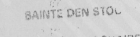

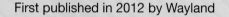

First published in 2012 by Wayland

Copyright © Wayland 2012

Wayland
338 Euston Road
London NW1 3BR

Wayland Australia
Level 17/207 Kent Street
Sydney NSW 2000

Editor: Debbie Foy
Designer: Lisa Peacock
Photographer: Ian Garlick
Proofreader/indexer: Sarah Doughty
Consultant: Sean Connolly

British Library Cataloguing in Publication Data

Professor Cook's fascinating fruits.
1. Cooking (Fruit)--Juvenile literature.
2. Fruit-- Composition--Juvenile literature.
I. Fascinating fruits
641.6'4-dc23

ISBN: 978 0 7502 6884 4

Printed in China

Wayland is a division of Hachette
Children's Books,
an Hachette UK Company.
www.hachette.co.uk

Contents

Professor Cook's Incredible Edibles!   04

Tropical fruit with goo-ey chocolate dip   06

Incredible edible tye-dye ices   08

Icy watermelon fruit slices   10

Hot pineapple 'lollies'   12

Super blueberry cheesecake   14

Wobbly strawberry mousse   16

'Magic' apple & blackberry pudding   18

Ice bowl fruit salad   20

Nicey slicey summer fruit jelly   22

Homemade yoghurt with fruit squish   24

Instant frozen yoghurt   26

Sticky licky banoffee cones   28

Professor Cook's glossary   30

Index & useful websites   32

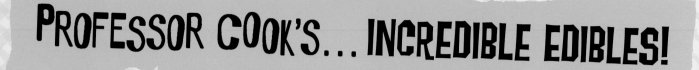

PROFESSOR COOK'S... INCREDIBLE EDIBLES!

ARE you hungry to LEARN MORE about your food?

Have you ever wondered why some foods behave the way they do? For example, have you ever considered how jellies or mousses set into their amazing wobbly shape? Or how a chocolate dip stays runny instead of setting hard?

Have you ever wondered what happens when fruit is frozen or how bananas can help ripen other fruit? Why we need to eat 5 fruits and vegetables a day or even how yoghurt contains friendly bacteria?

You can find the answers to these questions and more by joining Professor Cook's team to make instant frozen yoghurt, hot pineapple 'lollies', strawberry mousse with the wobble factor or tropical fruit with goo-ey chocolate dip!

HAPPY ~~EXPERIMENTING~~ COOKING!

PROFESSOR COOK'S KITCHEN RULE BOOK

→ Wash your hands before you start cooking and after handling raw stuff, like meat

→ Mop up spills as soon they happen

→ Use oven gloves for handling hot dishes straight from the oven

→ Listen up! Take care with sharp knives. Don't walk around with them!

→ Switch off the oven or cooker top when you have finished cooking

→ Use separate chopping boards for vegetables and meat

→ Raw and cooked foods should be kept separately in the fridge

→ Don't forget to tidy up the kitchen afterwards! No brainer, huh?

ABBREVIATIONS

g = grammes

tsp = teaspoon

tbsp = tablespoon

ml = millilitres

°C = degrees Celsius

HOT GOODS!

WHEN YOU SEE THIS WARNING SIGN AN ADULT'S HELP MAY BE NEEDED!

The 'Science Bits'

Believe it or not, cooking involves a lot of science! The Science Bits that accompany each of Professor Cook's delicious recipes answer all the mysteries about food that you have ever wanted to know. They also explore some of the interesting, unusual or quirky ways that our food often behaves!

TROPICAL FRUIT WITH GOO-EY CHOCOLATE DIP

Rich with choccy-ness this dip is the perfect complement to fresh and tangy tropical fruits. But what makes the dip stay goo-ey enough for you and your pals to keep coming back for more (and more)?

Step 1

Soak 12 wooden skewers in water for 25 minutes, to stop them burning when they go under a hot grill.

Step 2

Peel the kiwi fruit and pineapple and cut into chunks. De-hull the strawberries. Slice the star fruit and brush with lemon juice. Cut a slice from either side of the mango and discard the stone. Cut a criss-cross pattern into the flesh, turn inside out and cut away the mango cubes.

Stuff you need:

2 kiwi fruit
1/4 fresh pineapple
8 strawberries
1 star fruit
1 tbsp lemon juice
1 large ripe mango
Juice of 1/2 lemon
8 tbsp runny honey
8 tbsp milk
8 tbsp double cream
225g dark chocolate, broken into squares

Serves 4

HOT GOODS!

6

Step 3

Thread the fruit onto the pointed end of each skewer.

THE STAR FRUIT IS AN EXCELLENT SOURCE OF ASCORBIC ACID (VITAMIN C), IMPORTANT IN KEEPING BONES, TEETH AND SKIN HEALTHY!

The Science Bit

What makes the chocolate stay runny?

Melted chocolate usually sets, agreed? It's an example of a reversible change because chocolate melts, sets solid, then melts again. But here, double cream, honey and milk are added. The fats in the cream and milk combine with the cocoa butter, a vegetable fat in the chocolate. This combo of fats can produce a (WARNING: science word coming up!) eutectic system, which, in simple terms, means the chocolate stays runny!

Step 4

Put the honey, milk, double cream and chocolate in a small saucepan and heat gently over a low heat, stirring continuously until melted. Pour into a small bowl and serve with the fruit skewers.

INCREDIBLE EDIBLE TIE-DYE ICES

Who said you can only tie-dye clothes? Why not try lollies instead! They are packed full of juicy blackberries all wrapped up in a creamy 'brain-freezing' yoghurt!

Stuff you need:

85g fresh blackberries
Finely grated rind and juice of 1 lemon
4 tbsp icing sugar
300ml vanilla or natural yoghurt

Makes 4 lollies

Step 1

Place the blackberries and 1 tbsp lemon juice into a bowl and mash with a fork.

Step 2

Mix together the remaining lemon juice, lemon rind icing sugar and yoghurt.

BLACKBERRIES ARE high in Anti-oxidants called anthocyanins, which give them their dark colour!

Step 3

Drop a few spoonfuls of yoghurt mixture into **4 x 100ml** ice lolly moulds, then add a spoonful of blackberry mixture. Keep doing this until you have used up all the mixture and filled all the moulds.

Step 4

Push a wooden skewer into each lolly mould to stir up the mixtures a little. Cover the lolly moulds with their lids and freeze for at least 12 hours or overnight.

The Science Bit

What exactly _is_ brain freeze?

Brain freeze is the pain you feel when you eat freezing cold food such as an ice cream. When cold food touches the roof of your mouth it makes the blood vessels shrink or constrict. The sharp pain that you can get is caused by the blood rushing back into the blood vessels in order to heat the blood up again. Luckily, brain freeze usually lasts only about 30 seconds!

ICY WATERMELON FRUIT SLICES

There's nothing more refreshing than a slice of watermelon on a hot summer's day. So why not try our icy watermelon sorbet version!

Stuff you need:

1 small watermelon, halved
75g caster sugar
1 medium egg white
75g blueberries

Serves 8

Step 1

Scoop out the flesh from the watermelon halves leaving the shell intact. Roughly chop the flesh.

Step 2

Place the watermelon and sugar into a food processor and whizz to a slushy puree. Pour into a freezer-proof container and freeze for **4** hours until semi-frozen.

The Science Bit

Why add egg whites to sorbet?

Adding egg white to your sorbet help to give it a more creamy consistency and adds volume and texture. It also helps to stabilize the mixture (as an emulsifier). Emulsifying the mixture means that you can keep it in the freezer for longer!

Step 3

Use a fork to break up any large ice crystals. Whisk the egg white until stiff and fold into the frozen mixture. Add the blueberries. Spoon the semi-frozen mixture into one half of the watermelon shell. Cover with clingfilm and freeze overnight. Remove from the freezer 20 minutes before serving.

Stuff you need:

12 bamboo skewers
1 ripe pineapple, peeled
25g butter
25g light muscovado sugar
Finely grated rind of 1 lime
Chopped pistachio nuts

Makes 12

HOT GOODS!

SPEED UP THE RIPENING OF A PINEAPPLE by STANDING IT UPSIDE DOWN ON ITS LEAFY END!

Sticky and really juicy, these caramelized hot 'lollies' are even tastier when dipped in chopped pistachios!

Step 1

Soak the skewers in cold water for 25 minutes to stop them burning under the grill. Halve the pineapple lengthways and then cut each half into six long, thin wedges. Push each piece of pineapple onto a wooden skewer.

HOT PINEAPPLE 'LOLLIES'

Mix the butter, sugar and lime rind together to make a smooth paste.

Step 3

Heat a griddle pan until smoking and add the pineapple skewers. Cook for 2 minutes on each side until slightly charred. Dot the pineapple with the butter mixture and cook for a further minute until the sugar mixture has dissolved.

The Science Bit

Why is pineapple a jelly's worst enemy?

While pineapple is a deliciously nutritious fruit packed with vitamin C and fibre, it also contains an enzyme called bromelain, which acts to digest protein. So, if you add pineapple to a fruit jelly it simply won't set because the bromelain will act on the gelatine proteins and break them down!

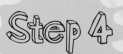

Sprinkle with pistachio nuts if liked and serve warm.

SUPER BLUEBERRY CHEESECAKE

One slice will not be enough! Crisp on the bottom, refreshing and creamy in the middle and super fruity on the top. Triple wow!

Stuff you need:

150g coconut biscuits
85g butter
225g caster sugar
Finely grated rind and juice of 2 limes
500g low fat soft curd cheese or quark
300ml double cream
1 x 7g sachet powdered gelatine
250g fresh blueberries

Serves 8

Step 1

Break up the biscuits and whizz in a food processor to make fine crumbs. Melt the butter in a saucepan and stir in the crumbs to coat evenly. Line the base of a 23cm springform cake tin with greaseproof paper. Press the biscuit mixture firmly into the base of the tin. Chill for 10 minutes in the fridge.

Step 2

In a large bowl mix together 150g of the caster sugar, lime zest and half the lime juice, curd cheese and double cream until well combined.

14

Step 3

Sprinkle the gelatine over 3 tbsp of warm water in a small bowl. Leave for 5 minutes. Place the bowl over a pan of hot water and heat until the gelatine has dissolved. Allow to cool for 5 minutes.

Step 4

Drizzle the dissolved gelatine into the creamy cheese mixture and whisk. Pour over the biscuit base and chill for 2-3 hours until set.

Step 5

Place the remaining sugar, lime juice and blueberries into a saucepan and heat gently until the sugar has dissolved and the blueberries are just releasing their juice. Remove the cheesecake from its tin and pour over the blueberry sauce to serve.

The Science Bit

Why do we add lime?

Lime adds a sharp citrus flavour and its acidity is a good partner to a rich, creamy cheesecake. Plus, scientists believe that our taste buds sense some flavours more strongly if they are offset by other flavours. So, we appreciate the cheesecake even more because it is combined with sour lime!

WOBBLY STRAWBERRY MOUSSE

What is packed full of sweet and nutritious strawberries but is high on the wobble factor? It's our amazing strawberry mousse! Move over jelly...

Step 1

Brush the inside of a 600ml jelly mould with oil. Place the gelatine leaves in a bowl and pour over 150ml cold water. Leave to stand for 5 minutes.

Stuff you need:

1 tsp vegetable oil
5 gelatine leaves
600g strawberries, hulled and quartered
150g icing sugar
450ml double cream
Fresh strawberries and mint leaves, to decorate

Serves 6-8

Did you know? THERE ARE about 200 SEEDS in EVERY STRAWBERRY!

Step 2

Place the strawberries and icing sugar into a food processor and whizz to a smooth puree. Sieve the strawberry mixture into a large bowl to create a smooth sauce.

Step 3

Gently warm the cream in a saucepan. Drain the gelatine and add the softened leaves to the cream. Stir until dissolved. Whisk in the strawberry puree, then pour into the jelly mould. Chill overnight.

Step 4

Dip the sides of the jelly mould into a bowl of warm water for about 30 seconds. Lift out of the water and cover with a plate. Turn the mould and the plate over and lift the mould away from the pudding. Decorate with fresh strawberries and mint.

The Science Bit

What creates the wobble factor?

It's gelatine! When heated gelatine becomes soluble, but when cooled it forms a gel. This gel acts as a kind of protein 'mesh' that traps water from the other liquids present in the recipe. This is a reversible process, as the gelatine will melt on heating but when cooled will reform again.

'MAGIC' APPLE & BLACKBERRY PUDDING

Try this fabulously fruity pudding with a delicious sauce that appears - as if by magic!

Stuff you need:

450g cooking apples, peeled, and cut into thick slices
225g blackberries
150g caster sugar
25g softened butter
25g plain flour
Finely grated rind and juice of 1 lemon
2 medium eggs, separated
150ml milk
25g flaked almonds
Icing sugar, to dust

Serves 6

HOT GOODS!

Step 1

Preheat the oven to 190°C/fan 170°C/gas mark 5. Put the apples and blackberries into an ovenproof dish and sprinkle with 50g of the sugar.

Step 2

Cream the butter and remaining sugar until pale and fluffy. Stir in the flour, lemon rind and juice, egg yolks and milk and beat until smooth. Don't worry if your mixture looks curdled!

Step 3

Whisk the egg whites until stiff and fold them into the lemon mixture. Spoon over the fruit to cover. Sprinkle over the flaked almonds.

Step 4

Place the ovenproof dish into a large roasting tin and very carefully pour boiling water until it reaches halfway up the sides of the ovenproof dish. Transfer to the oven and bake for 45-50 minutes. Dust with icing sugar and serve warm.

The Science Bit

What causes the 'magic' sauce?

The magic sauce is the result of the ingredients being denatured (or changed) in a chemical reaction. It's the acid in the lemon juice that helps them change in different ways. The proteins in the eggs and milk break down and release air (causing the pudding mixture to rise) but the cell walls of the fruits break down, making them more liquid. And that's magic!

Stuff you need:

For the ice bowl:
Small handful blueberries
1 kiwi fruit, sliced
1 star fruit, sliced
4 Gerbera flower heads
8 strawberries, halved
Handful ice cubes

For the fruit salad:
1 star fruit
1 lemon, halved
1/2 small melon, cut into chunks
125g seedless red grapes
1 kiwi fruit, peeled and chopped
300g tinned mandarin oranges
1 small papaya, peeled and chopped
100ml white grape juice

Serves 4-6

Pop on your gloves to make this wonderful icy creation to hold a tasty fruit salad. Brrrr...!

The Science Bit
What is dry ice?

Dry ice is NOT used in this recipe but it is still fascinating to know about! Dry ice is frozen carbon dioxide (CO_2) and is often used to preserve perishable items such a fruit. Fruits frozen with dry ice will thaw out to be firm instead of soggy or waterlogged!

ICE BOWL FRUIT SALAD

Step 1

For the ice bowl, fill a 2.4-litre glass mixing bowl two-thirds full with water. Place a 1.2-litre glass mixing bowl into the centre of the water. Secure with sticky tape so that the smaller bowl is central and the rims are level. Push the fruit and flowers into the water. Add ice cubes to keep them submerged. Freeze overnight.

Step 2

For the fruit salad, carefully slice the star fruit and squeeze over the lemon juice. Combine the melon, grapes, kiwi and oranges with the papaya, star fruit and grape juice. Chill until ready to use.

Step 3

Remove the bowls from the freezer. Fill the smaller one with warm water to and ease it out. Turn the bowl over. Pour warm water over the back of the larger bowl until the ice bowl inside releases. Place it onto a serving plate, add the fruit salad and serve!

NICEY SLICEY SUMMER FRUIT JELLY

This summer jelly is jam-packed with fruity goodness. You will be well on your way to your 5 a-day!

Step 1

Add 250ml water to the sugar and heat gently in a pan, stirring until the sugar dissolves. Bring to a boil and boil rapidly for 1 minute. Add the apple and raspberry, and the lemon juices.

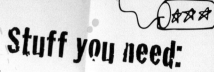

Stuff you need:

75g caster sugar
250ml clear fresh apple and raspberry juice
3 tbsp lemon juice
5 gelatine leaves
2 nectarines, chopped
225g raspberries
225g redcurrants

Serves 6

HOT GOODS!

RASPBERRIES COME IN MANY COLOURS. THERE ARE BLACK, PURPLE AND EVEN GOLDEN RASPBERRIES!

Step 2

Soften the gelatine in 150ml cold water. Leave for 2-3 minutes. Stand the bowl over a pan of simmering water for 2-3 minutes until the gelatine dissolves. Then add the gelatine to the juice mixture and stir.

Step 3

Place the nectarines, raspberries and redcurrants into a 1.2-litre nonstick loaf tin and mix gently. Pour over the gelatine mixture to cover and allow to set overnight.

What is your '5 a-day'?

Scientists have shown that eating at least 5 portions of fruit and vegetables each day has important health benefits and can help to prevent heart disease and some cancers. Fresh, frozen, dried and tinned fruit and veg can count as part of your 5 a-day!

Step 4

To release the jelly from the loaf tin, carefully dip the tin into warm water for 30 seconds. Position a plate over the top of the jelly and quickly turn the plate over. Lift the loaf tin off. Ta-dah!

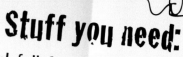

Stuff you need:

500ml full fat milk
25g dried milk powder
3 tbsp 'live' natural yoghurt
85g dried apricots, halved
50g raisins
50g dried cherries
1 fruit teabag
1 split vanilla pod
1 red apple, cored and sliced
Runny honey, to serve

Serves 4

HOT GOODS!

Did you know that some yoghurt is a living culture? Why not try making our homemade yoghurt recipe for a totally wholesome breakfast?

Step 1

Place the milk and milk powder into a saucepan and whisk until well combined. Place over the lowest heat and allow to warm gently without boiling.

HOMEMADE YOGHURT WITH FRUIT SQUISH

Step 2

Stir in the yoghurt and pour into a flask. Set aside and leave overnight until set.

Step 3

Place the fruit into a pan with the teabag, vanilla pod and 150ml boiling water and leave to go cold.

Step 4

Drain the fruit, discard the teabag and remove the vanilla pod. Very carefully remove the seeds from the pod and stir into the yoghurt. Divide the yoghurt between 4 glasses. Spoon over the soaked fruit and add apple slices. Drizzle with honey to serve.

The Science Bit

How is yoghurt a 'living culture'?

Milk (the main ingredient of yoghurt) contains a natural sugar, lactose. Naturally occurring bacteria feed off lactose and produce lactic acid. When bacteria have warmth (such as in the flask) they breed and multiply, producing more lactic acid. Lactic acid changes the texture and taste of the milk by a process called denaturing. Hey presto! We have yoghurt.

Stuff you need:

500g bag frozen mixed summer fruits
400g Greek yoghurt
Finely grated rind and juice of 1 large orange
2 tbsp icing sugar
Small handful fresh cherries
Mint sprigs, to decorate

Serves 6

CHERRIES ARE RICH IN MELATONIN WHICH HAS A SOOTHING AND RELAXING EFFECT ON THE BRAIN!

The Science Bit

Does freezing alter your fresh fruit?

Fresh fruit retains a lot of its nutrients if frozen quickly after picking. But fresh fruit tends to lose its shape when defrosted. This happens because the cells are broken when the water in them expands as it freezes. So frozen fruits are ideal for cooking or blending into recipes like frozen yoghurt!

INSTANT FROZEN YOGHURT

This ready-before-you-know-it frozen yoghurt is a healthy alternative to ice cream since it contains half the fat and is stuffed full of healthy fruit!

Step 1

Place the frozen fruits, yoghurt, orange rind and juice and icing sugar into a food processor. Whizz up the mixture (using a spatula to scrape down the sides of the food processor) until totally smooth.

Step 2

Spoon the yoghurt mixture into serving glasses. Top with fresh cherries and mint sprigs to serve.

STICKY LICKY BANOFFEE CONES

Whizz up an banana-licious treat in a cone! Bananas are healthy and taste good but they also have other very special uses...

Stuff you need:

- 4 bananas
- 4 wafer ice cream cones
- 2 tbsp dulce de leche (thick caramel sauce)
- ½ tsp vanilla extract
- 4 tbsp caster sugar
- 150ml buttermilk
- 8 dried banana chips
- 2 tbsp grated chocolate

Makes 4 cones

Step 1

Peel 3 bananas and cut into thick slices. Arrange on a baking tray and freeze for at least 2 hours until solid.

Step 2

While keeping the bananas frozen, peel and chop the remaining banana and push a quarter of it into each cone. Stand the cones upright in a jug to help you. Add 1 tbsp of caramel sauce into each cone.

Step 3

Remove the bananas from the freezer and whizz up in a food processor with the vanilla, sugar and half the buttermilk. Scrape down

the sides using a spatula, add the remaining buttermilk and whizz again until smooth.

Step 4

Spoon the ice cream into the cones, top with dried banana, a drizzle of caramel sauce and dust with chocolate.

The Science Bit

How are bananas useful?

To speed up the ripening of fruits such as avocados, mangoes, peaches and pears, place a ripe banana and the unripe fruit into a paper bag. The banana emits a gas called ethylene which acts a a signal to other fruit to start ripening. How useful is that?

PROFESSOR COOK'S GLOSSARY

ANTHOCYANINS pigments that give many fruits their dark colour

ANTI-OXIDANTS substances found in many fruits and vegetables that help to prevent damage in the body and repair cells

ASCORBIC ACID a form of vitamin C, mainly found in fruits and vegetables

BACTERIA single-celled organisms that are found in the air, in water, in food and many other places, some of which cause disease

BROMELAIN an enzyme found in pineapple and kiwi fruits that breaks down the protein, gelatine

BUTTERMILK a slightly sour liquid left after butter has been churned, often used in baking

CELLS tiny units that make up all living things

CULTURE the growth of organisms

DENATURING to remove or alter the natural qualities of something

EMULSIFY to create a mixture of two or more liquids (which would not normally mix)

ENZYMES molecules that control chemical reactions in living organisms

ETHYLENE a gas produced by bananas that causes other fruits to ripen

EUTECTIC this describes a mixture of chemical substances that melts at a lower temperature than either of the mixed substances

FIBRE food items that add bulk to our diets such as cereals, fruits and vegetables

GEL a semi-solid material

GELATINE a setting agent used in many puddings and desserts

GRIDDLE PAN a heavy cast-iron pan that creates chargrilled 'lines' across your food

HORMONE a chemical produced by living things that help make changes in cells

LACTIC ACID an acid present in sour milk and also produced in our muscles when we exercise

MELATONIN a hormone produced in the body that is involved in regulating the sleeping and waking cycles

NUTRIENTS these are substances found in our food and drink, including carbohydrates, minerals, proteins and vitamins

PRESERVATIVE substances added to food to prevent it from spoiling

REVERSIBLE CHANGE a chemical process that can be reversed (or turned back)

SOLUBLE describes substances that can be easily dissolved in a liquid

SPRINGFORM CAKE TIN a cake tin with removable sides and base

WHISK to beat with a light, rapid motion

INDEX

5 a-day 4, 22, 23

acidity 15
anthocyanins 8
antioxidants 8
ascorbic acid 7

bacteria 4, 25
bananas 4, 28, 29
blood vessels 9
brain freeze 8, 9
breakfast 24
bromelain 13

cancers 23
caramelization 12, 13
carbon dioxide 20
cheesecake 14, 15
chocolate 4, 6, 7, 28, 29
cold food 9

denaturing 19, 25
dip 4, 6, 7

dry ice 20

egg whites 11, 19
enzymes 13

freezing 4, 8, 9, 10, 11, 20, 21, 26, 27, 28, 29
fridges 5

gelatine 13, 14, 15, 16, 17

heart disease 23
hygiene 5

ice cream 9, 27, 29

jelly 4, 13, 22, 23

lactose 25
lime 15
living culture 24, 25
lollies 4, 8, 9, 12, 13
melting 7

mousse 4, 16, 17

nutrients 13, 26

oven gloves 5

preservative 11, 20
protein 13, 17, 19

ripening 12, 29

sorbet 10, 11
spills 5

tie-dye 8, 9

vitamin C 7, 13

yoghurt 4, 8, 9, 24, 25, 26, 27

USEFUL WEBSITES

www.spatulatta.com
Get some basic cooking skills under your belt, with step-by-step video recipes and a recipe box that includes options for cooking a meal by choosing a basic ingredient, a type of food, occasion or particular diet.

www.yummyscience.co.uk
Super-fun science projects to try out in the kitchen using everyday foods. Grow your own crystals with salt, test out the toasting properties of bread or make your own honeycomb toffee. Some of these recipes call for an adult's help, so always make sure you let an adult know before you start.

www.exploratorium.edu/cooking
Find out how a pinch of curiosity can improve your cooking! Explore recipes, activities and webcasts that will improve your understanding of the science behind food and cooking.

Discover some more incredible edibles with PROFESSOR COOK and the team!

Smashing Snacks
9780750268516

Pop-tastic popcorn
Smashing caramel shards
Ice cream in a bag
Cheese-and-ham-o-rama!
Homemade beans on toast
Oat-so yummy power cookies
'No-cry' onion bhajis
Double-dipped mallow cookies
Mini superhero pies!
Gold bullion honeycomb bars!
Pink fizz-bomb lemonade
Big dipper breadsticks
Professor Cook's glossary
Index

Mind-Blowing Bakes
9780750268837

Oozing crust pizza
Stack 'em high cheesy puff pie
Exploding cupcakes
Stained glass cookies
Crimson velvet whoopie pies!
Very berry choco meringues
Kitchen sink pot pies
Hot ice cream sparkle
Super seedy flowerpot bread
Choc pops
Black and blue buns
Squidy widgy custard tarts
Professor Cook's glossary
Index

Dynamite Dinners
9780750268523

Sticky chicky burger stacks
Tex Mex taco salad bowl
Incredible edible bowl soup!
Posh fish 'n' chips 'n' dip!
Pimp your burger!
Finger lickin' chicken satay
Japan-easy tuna rolls
Tongue-tingling sweet and sour noodles
Thirsty couscous cakes!
Scrambly egg fried rice
Superfood cannelloni
Chilli with a deep, dark secret
Professor Cook's glossary
Index

Fascinating Fruits
9780750268844

Tropical fruit with goo-ey chocolate dip
Incredible edible tie-dye lollies
Icy watermelon slices
Hot caramelised pineapple lollies
Super blueberry cheesecake
Homemade yoghurt with fruit squish
'Magic' apple and blackberry pudding
Nicey slicey summer fruit jelly
Wobbly strawberry mousse
Ice bowl fruit salad
Instant frozen yoghurt
Sticky licky banoffee cones
Professor Cook's glossary
Index

WAYLAND